The Night of Mary

Sharing Heaven and a Call to Grace

SHARON HOUGHTON

BALBOA.
PRESS
A DIVISION OF HAY HOUSE

Balboa Press books may be ordered through booksellers or by contacting:

Balboa Press
A Division of Hay House
1663 Liberty Drive
Bloomington, IN 47403
www.balboapress.com
1 (877) 407-4847

Because of the dynamic nature of the Internet, any web addresses or
links contained in this book may have changed since publication and
may no longer be valid. The views expressed in this work are solely those
of the author and do not necessarily reflect the views of the publisher,
and the publisher hereby disclaims any responsibility for them.

The author of this book does not dispense medical advice or prescribe the use
of any technique as a form of treatment for physical, emotional, or medical
problems without the advice of a physician, either directly or indirectly. The
intent of the author is only to offer information of a general nature to help
you in your quest for emotional and spiritual well-being. In the event you use
any of the information in this book for yourself, which is your constitutional
right, the author and the publisher assume no responsibility for your actions.

Any people depicted in stock imagery provided by Thinkstock are
models, and such images are being used for illustrative purposes only.
Certain stock imagery © Thinkstock.

Printed in the United States of America.

ISBN: 978-1-4525-2174-9 (sc)
ISBN: 978-1-4525-2175-6 (e)

Balboa Press rev. date: 11/12/2014

Foreword

Always considering myself a bit of a rebel when it came to society and the norms of fitting into what others expected, it is not surprising that I tell this story as amazed and perplexed as you will be.

It is a recounting of my past 15 years of a glorious Gift that was bestowed upon me that takes a great deal of introspection and self-awareness to explore. Maybe I need the reader to explore it with me in order that a true understanding can be achieved........ Even by me.

Being born in a middle class family in a an average neighborhood in the Midwest, every Sunday my father would tell my brothers and sisters to "get to church" and I recall early memories of running down the stairs only to have him tell me to change my clothes or to don a longer skirt . My Father was a very religious man and had been raised in a large Irish Catholic family. As a successful funeral director, Dad knew life and he knew death in its most basic form. I will always recall him saying, "You can tell a person by their funeral".

To my Father, it was the development of relationships, business associates and friends that defined the impact people had made in their lives. How was a person loved and who were his family and friends? What was his career? And the list goes on. My father took a deep interest in the purpose of people and how they fit into the grand scheme of society.

Dad was 6'5" tall, a white-haired man and warm to the touch. He had a laugh that was not to be forgotten. He looked so Irish that his nickname was "Mickey", with the Irish temper to accompany it on many occasions. He worked hard and loved everyone in our family and, most importantly, did the very best he could for all of us in his own special and personal way.

So the story I am to tell is a true one, told of integrity and purpose. It is a story that begins with the love of my Father and ends with an understanding of the mystery and the Glory of God.

The date is Aug 2, 1998 and many years had passed. I was a grown woman, working for a local TV station in Columbus, Ohio selling advertising and married to my high school sweetheart. I gave birth to an adorable son, Luke, and we moved to a 90 acre farm in Southern Ohio.

As a busy wife, mother, and sales professional, making ends meet was my principal endeavor - just like most families in America. All seemed happy and content until the phone call that would change not only my life, but hundreds of lives in the years to come.

I was on my way to Toledo, Ohio to meet a client for business purposes. It was a sunny summer day when my mobile phone rang. Long before being known as a "cell", this was a big deal and I was surprised to hear it make its funny ring tone. Through the static, I recognized my Dad's voice which sounded a bit strained. He told me that he had just seen his doctor and had very "disconcerting news" to use his exact words. Dad told me that his doctor had diagnosed an aneurysm on his aorta, a major blood supply artery in his body.

As this information was sinking in, it dawned on me in a very peculiar way that it had something to do with his heart. He added that, "Once they check my heart, then they will operate and put a stent in my aorta and I should be ok. I wanted to let you know what was going on".

I apprehensively replied as any person would that this sounded serious and asked the basic questions as to pain, type of surgery, recovery and seriousness. I recall asking him questions about his heart and he encouraged me that all would be ok. Still, the fears that are normal to everyone receiving this type of news began to rise. We had always been close and the thought of any type of surgical procedure sent my mind racing into great concern.

Although terribly pre-occupied with this news, I completed my meeting with the client and began my trip home to Columbus. Heading down Rt. 23, I noticed a sign for a church that I recognized from childhood. It was known as the Sorrowful Mother Shrine that was located in the very small rural town of Carey Ohio.

Years before, when my Grandfather and I would visit family relatives in Michigan we would always stop at the Cary church. It stood for centuries as one of the oldest Catholic Churches in the country, but to me it was more, a place of enlightenment and solidarity for my family. Amongst the very old stained glass windows and the structure of old, I felt the peace within that had granted the same to so many souls that had worshipped there over the decades.

Grandfather and I would pray during our visit and enjoy the quiet time together and the serenity that the church invokes. We always were fascinated with its beauty and ancient design and even lit candles together in its main sanctum. Often we walked together through the shrine area that was always adorned with those remembrances of those passed and the feeling of those that still existed with their peace and love that remained.

At one point I had learned that "Carey", as I had come to call it, was a shrine that was internationally recognized as having been the site responsible for many healings and was a spiritual deity who's Priests focused their belief on a special attention for this church toward the love of Mary, the Mother of Jesus.

While driving that day, without the slightest hesitation, I chose to take that exit and drive over to the Carey site. Not only wanting a break from the drive and to relive old memories of the church, I felt compelled to say a prayer for my Father and take the opportunity to calm my mind a bit.

I recall that it was around 3pm in the afternoon and no one was in the church. But as a shrine the doors were open and I went in. I remembered the beautiful statues of Jesus and Mary, the glory of their presence and the beauty of their peacefulness that literally glowed within my heart and deep within my soul.

The elegant stained glass of the Church was prettier than I remembered from childhood.

I walked very humbly to the statue of the Mother Mary.

As learned as a child, I placed offerings and lit candles as I bowed before her and recited prayers. I also was sure to leave my dollar in the Church's box to pay for the candle I was about to light. I looked at the statue and in a humble sort of way I said this prayer.

"I know Mary that you all are very busy, but if you could ask God to let me know my Dad will be okay, I would appreciate it." I looked to the statue, humbled and reveling in her glory, then rose and left the church.

I didn't expect an answer, I just knew I had to get on my way back home to continue my busy life.

Once again, at the time, I had no idea as to what would yet transpire that would bring this simple act into the forefront of quite an elaborate and enlightening series of events that would greatly effect my life.

The Night of Mary

It was mid evening when I arrived home and I don't recall really saying much about my stop at the Carey Shrine other than just mentioning it in passing to my husband. I fixed dinner, completed the laundry obligations for the upcoming week, and went to bed that night tired from the trip and the news of the day.

I anticipated an easy sleep and then incredible events began to unfold that are, to this day, still as exciting and amazing to relive as they were at the time of my experience that night. Even to recount the story for you, my reader, envelops me in a divine presence that is difficult to describe.

I was awakened during the night when I felt a "shaking" on my right shoulder that I had first thought was my young son trying to wake me in a vigorous way and that he needed help. I jumped up to see what the problem was and saw that he wasn't standing there.

As I turned my head, there She was. I was instantly shocked to see a clear apparition of the Virgin Mary on bright white clouds, her hands in the grace position by her side with beams of light flowing from her hands. She is BEAUTIFUL and her radiant glory was overwhelming!

The details of this experience are clear and distinct and I will never forget her brown hair with a blue mantle on her head and her wondrous skin and perfect nose. She wore a gray long dress and was barefoot and was floating in my bedroom on churning white clouds. The reality just can't be described.

I know I'm awake! I slapped my hands as I stared at her glory. I hit my face as I stared at her glory. Wide wake!

I was in awe as Mary spoke to me in Her sweet loving voice and said, "I am here to answer your prayers. I am here to say that you will bring me two rosaries". Mary continued by saying, "the first he will make it through the surgery, the second will be at his death". I was frozen in wonder as she showed me an image of my Dad's gravesite with my son and me in an embrace standing near. She then said, "You are receiving a great grace!" Then She left on the beautiful white clouds without making a sound.

What just happened? I began again, as the room returned to quiet, telling myself that it was just a dream but what a glorious dream. But I was totally awake and alert and can vividly and accurately recall every single detail of this event. How am I going to explain what I just experienced or should it even have an explanation at all? It should be said at this point that I was not scared or afraid, yet personally humbled and astonished.

The next day I went to work and I didn't say a word to anyone about my experience as I was still trying to come to grips with it in my own mind. How would I be perceived by my friends and business associates if I told them of this? Would people be amazed and excited like I was, or would it be suggested that I see a doctor?

While sorting this out in my mind and trying to focus on the normal tasks of the day, that now seemed so inconsequential, I decided to try and relax and allow the experience to settle a bit in my mind.

Of course, within just a few minutes, that strategy would change dramatically as a friend at work came up to me and said she had something for me. I was starting to understand that the "Gift" I was told about by Mary was just beginning. My friend handed me two Rosaries. One black and one white.

Then my friend told me that she had them delivered from Rome and I asked her why she gave me these rosaries. She simply replied that she, "had to get them for me". They were very nice and I explained to her what had happened the night before. She was as surprised as I was and listened intently to my account of the experience.

Ok- so let's recap, I go to a shrine, I say a prayer, I have visions of Mary on white clouds and the next day someone gives me two rosaries. I know what you are thinking – oh sure! At least I was. I went home that night and the doubting Thomas that

I was, I went to my bedroom and said with my finger pointing to the ceiling, "DO IT AGAIN if this is real".

Ok maybe I shouldn't have done that, maybe I was testing myself, my God, my vision.

Of course, nothing happened at that moment, however, my words were definitely heard. Later that night the Blessed Mother would again return to remove any and all doubt as to what was real. Once again, I was awakened by a shaking on my right shoulder hard.

I jerked up this time……….. Ready.

There She was on the beautiful white clouds, barefoot, hands in grace by her side, just as She had appeared the prior night. Her face, again, radiating elegantly and her voice so kind and sweet. This time smiling almost a giggle, She said, "Sharon it is true! You are receiving a great Grace! Now count to four."

I did as l was told and spoke, "one, two, three" and then found myself looking at the alarm clock for a second, "four". It was 12:34 that night. I quickly turned my head and she was gone. Gone on her clouds of Grace and beauty and leaving me, once again, spellbound and excited by the experience.

What is a Grace?

Of course the past two nights were heavy on my mind. What is Grace and what does she mean by this? And why was I chosen to experience these apparitions? I certainly was never a fierce student of Catholicism and, growing up, found most of the teachings boring while there were more exciting and fun things to do.

Of course I had heard the term "Grace" but just never explored the depth of its meaning. Simply put, Grace is a blessing, a gift from God, and It is what later would prove to be a way of life for me. A way to breathe and believe. It is warmth and joy and sadness all in one that gives one the ability to see events through the Holy Spirit. It is love and frustration and hope all mixed together. It is a blessing that for some reason I was chosen to receive through my visits by Mary.

My life changed overnight. I started having more dreams at night and these dreams would often come true the following day. That's when you know in your soul that something has happened to you. It took a long time to accept this but that would only be the beginning. This occurred night after night and I became acutely aware that the Grace bestowed upon me would forever change everything for me and how I perceived the world and people around me.

These "foretelling dreams" started to happen right away. From the effects of this experience I was changed within and given enlightenments that would continue to this day. So many of these messages, predictions, apparitions and even, at times, warnings would have the substance to be proven. Messages validated in the actions of others and even world events would manifest as I would be shown them in advance of there occurrence.

The responsibility of this "Gift" was becoming very clear.

My father collapsed 3 weeks later due to his aorta rupturing. Thank God Jeannine, my younger sister, was at his home at the time to call the squad and comfort him.

When the medics arrived, they immediately transported Dad to the hospital. By the time I arrived with other family members, they told us that the odds of pulling him through this weren't good. Dad was bleeding into his abdomen and the doctors suggested that we see Dad and comfort him the best as possible and to say "good bye" just in case the worst happened.

I walked into the room and held his hand and told him how much I loved him and that I would be there when he awoke from the surgery. Although very weak, he smiled and said that he loved me.

What I did next may sound strange but blame it on the events in my life at the time. I went to the rest room and stood in the bathroom pointing my finger at the ceiling and said, "YOU SAID HE WOULD BE OK AND I'M HOLDING YOU TO IT".

As I sat in the waiting room with my family it seemed like forever.

Finally, the surgeon came out to us and advised that Dad had made it through the surgery and was being taken to the Intensive Care Unit for recovery. A definite close call that shook our whole family and friends.

Several days later, I happened to be visiting Dad in ICU. He was sitting in the room and I stopped in on my break from work. "Checking on you," I said, as I popped into his small hospital room that was littered with many notes and cards encouraging a speedy recovery. The small TV was on and playing with the sound off. I was the only one in the room as I sat by his side to just be there.

Dad looked at me and said, "I need a rosary, can you get me one?"

Just like it was meant to be, I had the two rosaries right there in my purse that were given to me by my co-worker a couple days earlier. I asked if he wanted the white or black rosary and Dad chose the white one. In my heart, I knew that was the "first rosary", the rosary that Mary had spoken of in my apparition of Her. The first rosary that I brought to him and to her.

It made me upset but I knew that it was God's divine plan. Knowing this, however, did not make it any easier to accept. Dad and I spent some quality time that day although little was discussed.

As I walked from the hospital to my car that day, I reflected intently on the events that had unfolded over the past days and how life-changing they were becoming to me. It was difficult to define within myself whether being visited by the divine and having vivid dreams that came true was a good thing at all. Face it, this "gift" would carry a great responsibility for any person.

One thought in my mind, and I am sure it has crossed yours too, my reader, was a possible mental illness or anxiety developing from all my home and work stress and triggered by an aortic aneurysm of my father. This sounded plausible at the time so I made an appointment with my family doctor of 21 years in order to get a complete checkup. It would help to get a trusted opinion to just make sure all was well.

A complete physical usually gives the opportunity to discuss a variety of things with a doctor and I would just slip in the topic of seeing the Virgin Mary, blindly receiving rosaries, dreams that come true, and being "in tune" with the thoughts of others.

So I made the appointment and within a week or so met with my doctor. He initially asked why I thought I needed the appointment and I responded very curiously as to what I was "feeling from him". I simply stated "You went to a funeral yesterday, the man smoked himself to death and he says thanks for coming Doc".

It was instantly apparent by the amazed look on his face that he couldn't believe that I said it. He told me I was quite right and then we had a discussion where I explained what was happening. He confirmed later that indeed he was at a funeral of a family relative the day before and that lung cancer was the cause of his patient's demise.

I passed all my medical tests with flying colors and, according to my favorite doctor, was not going insane. He requested I stay in touch and monitor my feelings and events that might arise and keep him informed. He stated that I was slightly stressed but that no prescription was necessary.

Life moved forward.

My sister, Jenny, got married in 1998 and Dad was there to join us. How tremendous it was to have him participate in the wedding that was such a big event for my sister as well as the entire family.

Next came Christmas and New Years and it was 1999.

Dad began to have problems with his heart and they couldn't get the blood "numbers" stabilized right for surgery. Dad was at his home and functioning but moving slowly. He was waiting for April when they would do the bypass surgery on him to repair his heart. Dad had arterial blockage everywhere that with medical advancements today would be corrected fairly easily and ensure a higher quality of his remaining years.

Now we reach March 12th as we await the surgery scheduled for April and I am on my way to a hockey game in Newark Ohio. My son played on the team and provided exciting entertainment as their league was one of the highest ranked in the state.

I had just completed check-in at the hotel and was just settling in when I received a call from my Mother.

Even before answering, my awareness changed.

It was around 8pm when I heard my mother's voice. She sounded very different and was barely holding herself together as she told me that Dad had died.

I grabbed my overnight bag and the hockey gear and quickly left the hotel to head home. Tears ran down my face as I knew the loss of my father would be a difficult thing to accept and the pain that my family would all feel as they received "their calls" from my mother.

Thinking back, there was no reason to be flying in panic and shock but events of passing bring out emotions in all good human beings and I just wanted to see Dad one more time.

I called my in-laws and told them that Dad had passed and asked that they get to my Mom to provide some comfort and any help she might need.

Driving a little too quickly, I make my trip home in half the time. Not a divine event - just amazingly cooperative traffic lights. I was home in about 25 minutes and arrived just as the workers from the funeral home were about to take Dad. I was able to touch his hand one last time and attempt to transfer my loss into a quiet prayer that he find his way to his Savior.

As a part of life, so many people have to experience the loss of loved ones and the immediacy and the truth of the process of passing. I suppose, coming from a family of funeral directors, it might have been a bit easier for me in some ways .... probably not.

Mom asked me for a Rosary for his hands which was the second Rosary waiting in my purse.

A few days later, Dad's funeral ceremony was held and the attendance was amazing with the procession of cars to the cemetery stretching over a mile long. Dad received a Military sendoff with 21-gun salute, bagpipes, and even an aircraft flyover provided by the United States Air Force.

Dad was right, without a doubt, "you can tell a man by his funeral".

The Gift

At this point in my life, I began having so many visions, dreams coming true, and miracles every day. I was growing in a spiritual way fast and at times it was nearly overwhelming.

I didn't want to share my gift with anyone. I had a wanting to hide it and not wanting to be judged by others. Talk about opening yourself up for criticism. I mean what would people think? At the same thought, I wanted to share it with everyone. I wanted to let people know what I was experiencing and the truths and glories that lie in wait for us all.

Was there anyone else like me? I started to read, research, study the Bible, try and understand each item, segment, vision I was experiencing now on daily basis. I didn't see Mary on a daily basis, but I was experiencing Grace.

It manifested in many ways. I continued to have visions from The Blessed Mother Mary. Her Grace and words were very helpful and her visits were deep and meaningful. One in particular informed me that the veil has been lifted for me. That I would see the unseen. I would be under her mantle in my life. My journey was just beginning.

Life

Looking back, I have had so many experiences and wish I could make this enlightenment easier for everyone to grasp. Like everyone else, I am just as surprised by the blessings and Grace that I have received.

After those first weeks of confusion and wanting to pretend that nothing happened, the Grace got in the way. I started to see the unseen and continued having the truth-fulfilling dreams, still questioning my own psychology. I wanted to believe there was a medical reason for what was happening and met with more doctors, ministers, and even a psychologist.

Please prove me wrong, give me a pill and make this life of mine normal again. Each and every time I wanted them to prove me wrong, that didn't happen. With some amusement, I often told them more about themselves and their lives as they sat in amazement.

But that wasn't in God's plan. Each time I tried to dismiss my feelings and perceptions it proved the Grace stronger and more powerful. Many of the dreams and visions involved past events and I would seek out historical references and historians to prove what I was seeing was inaccurate in history.......... but it wasn't.

I continued for four years to prove, talk rationally, and disprove what I was now seeing on a daily basis. It finally made me smile as I began to truly accept that my experiences were truly a grace from God.

I do not pray for hours on end or immerse myself in Biblical verse. I do not pray for "signs" nor do I pray in the hopes to catch a glimmer of God's presence. I pray for love, success, hope, and health. For my family, friends, and all of humanity.

But I have to say it continues to lead me on a wild and wonderful ever-fulfilling journey. I have always been taught by my family to be loving and caring. I guess this is the basis for how my life is now.

I have met with so many people that have sought me out to discuss their lives. As I write this narrative, the number continues to grow in addition to articles and public speaking appearances.

They have come from all ages, backgrounds, economic and religious status seeking answers to their life questions and problems in their lives.

I have seen, heard, and tried to help them all. Yes, it gets hectic but I have learned that it isn't anything I can't handle. People often ask, "are you tired" nope not yet just busy. I guess that is the grace and the Holy Spirit working within me and in all of us.

I am not alone, I have a team to support me, a team of Angels, My holy Mother and my Lord. What a great team! We all have this team, I just see them.

It's a true blessing. The ability to weather the storm and see the unseen. To help and heal and teach people how to help themselves. It's available to all of us. Some find it scary and are fearful of things unknown or out of the ordinary. These fears merely represent their own insecurities and self-doubts.

Because if you had Grace you would know it's magnificent. It's a cherished gift that doesn't have a price. It brings peace and enlightenment in that storm I spoke of earlier.

It's ultimate love.

Visions

This is a very difficult subject for me. Over the years I have had so many experiences which you, my reader, will see. I had thought about going into individual detail on the visions I have had for myself and for others, however, I realize there is one dominate answer - and it may take time to get to the answer - but the answer is always the same.

It is a knowing.

Belief is something you want or have been taught. Knowing is taking a belief and without a doubt know that what you are seeing, feeling or experiencing is truth. I know now that what I have is for real. That the seeing of families, war, deceased, disease, is a knowing. I hope that after you read of some of the situations I have been placed in that you too will know....... and not just believe.

When I said I have had many apparitions, they are now too many to count. Some I keep very private and I don't speak of them unless asked. Then it's like a waterfall of information. People have asked me what Mary or Jesus looks like, I have an artist that has worked with me to best depict them the way I see them. I always see Mary and Jesus on white clouds. Mary is always in her gray simple dress and a beautiful pale blue Mantel or veil. She comes on the clouds barefoot, I get a feeling of calm, joy, peace and focus when these Divine visions appear.

I communicate with Her from my brain or words. She speaks in a most sweet calm tone as a mother is speaking to a child. She is as they say "full of Grace". Through the years she has shown me places of turmoil around the world and asks to pray. She has shown me and told me the rosary, to use it as a meditation on her Son. It is one of the beautiful weapons against evil in the world. She asks us to pray with family and friends. Mary, is a mother.

She has shown me along with her son the cross and I will describe that to you later in detail as I have seen the carrying and crucifixion of her son in a very dramatic apparition. I have seen Mary weep in agony of the pain and suffering at the cross. I have also seen her call her Angels to assist her in receiving souls for heaven.

She was given the title of Queen of Peace and Mother of the World at the Cross. She has been through the agony that many mothers today still suffer from. She has been threatened by being pregnant and having a child out of wedlock only to be rescued by the Grace of God and an angel to Joseph her spouse. She has had to flee countries while her family was threatened by a Government trying to destroy them. I think of the Three Wise men and how they looked so different.

When Mary gave birth to Jesus, she was given the Gold, Frankincense and Myrrh. But she was also given a cloak of Royal blue/Purple almost a pure indigo which signified the royalty of the family. She used the Gold for food and security, the Frankincense for healing and the Myrrh to treat any infections in her life. She was rescued again by God and this time the three Wise men with Angels guiding her path safely to exile in Egypt.

When Jesus was young, He disappeared and was missing for days, as a Mother you can only imagine the fear she had that He was lost. Mary found him in the temple meeting with leaders to discuss the world and their needs. Again, Mary was rescued by God. When Jesus and Mary were at a wedding in Cana, the Wedding party ran out of wine, and as it is said in the first miracle performed by Jesus, Mary told him to go make wine.

I find it curious and fascinating that Mary knew that he could.

She knew Her Son, His abilities and often stubborn ways, and knew He needed to do this. As She followed Her Son on His path to Holiness, Mary must have thought all would be well, never expecting the agony in the garden, the scourging as she watched Her son being tortured. The followers that had betrayed Him and the cruelty of carrying of a very heavy cross in the streets. She watched and agonized as He was crucified, and took Him to His burial site.

But God was there, He rescued Mary. He showed Her that He was alive and She ran to tell the Apostles with joy that He was alive. Mary was then taken again in exile where She was assumed into Heaven only to see the plan of God and Her Son. Mary was rescued yet again by God.

Why am I reminding you of this life of Mary? Simply, it has been an answer to so many when they are in a situation of agony and sorrow and despair. There is a passage in the bible where it says "where two or more pray in my name". Mary is always with her children who are alone, agonizing in fear and near death, ready to be with them as their second. Praying to her Son with you as a good Mother would do.

Mary is the Mother of the world and of you and I in the most loving spiritual way.

She is one of the most documented figures in historical religions and has been identified as having the ability to change the minds of people away from agony and into hope. She is always working for you as your Mother in heaven and spiritually here on Earth.

I have so many visions of Mary, but I know in my heart that She is here for all of us as She reaches out to comfort us and guide us as She would children in her life.

Mary has appeared and will continue to appear to people throughout existence. History records many witnessed, documented, and validated testimonies to her appearances and has led thousands of followers to spiritual centers of faith. Fatima, Lourdes, Medjugore, Garanbendal, Knock, only to name a few, have become well known as a result of Her apparitions.

I see her now each week and it is truly incredible.

Mary came slowly to me, but I have noticed of late, that she is appearing more often, telling me of the World and its agony. She also tells me of my life, family, and friends.

I know I am different than other visionaries of the world. I know they have set times of Day or Days of the Month that Mary is said to appear to them. It seems that I have a weekly private apparition unless at my Grotto. She is always with me at My Grotto.

I can't "call upon" Her or "channel her" as others often refer to how they communicate with Mary. She appears when necessary to me and She knows I will do my best to deliver the messages to those She has asked me to deliver them to.

I wonder, since she is able to do this to me, then why doesn't she just appear directly to the person. After asking this question countless times, I feel the answer lies in the delivery itself. I really don't believe most would hear or understand out of shock arising from the magnificence of her presence. It took me years to accept this beautiful Grace as a Knowing.

It has always been my assumption that many people, especially those in personal sorrow or crisis, need the extra touch of a "random" person to deliver Mary's messages to make it real and understandable for them. Someone who has no specific interest in the intended receiver other than to convey Mary's message. It is at this point that the message becomes their own to digest and comprehend. Much like an interpreter of languages, it is not my place to adapt or change the message but to make it understandable to each specific person it is intended.

Although I quote very little Biblical verse, some just applies so well. For example, as it has been said at Pentecost; "some hear thunder", simply meaning that some individuals will actually hear the grace and feel the love and others just plain won't. This is not said in any way to diminish the faith of the latter group…..it just appears to be the way things are.

Yes, my reader, I will always try to explain the best that I can verbalize so that you can get a better understanding of my experiences but I know it will always have its elements of mystery and confusion. That concept seems to come with the territory.

Often times, I have to give forth a great effort to get Mary's messages and knowledge to what might be referred to as the "hardened person" to allow the peace within the message to penetrate their heart. Again, I am just her messenger, a person sent by Mary to reach the person who may be experiencing the agony like Mary once endured.

Mary, like a good Mother, is trying to rescue her children with love and by providing direction and understanding to help them in their lives within Her messages.

She is using many messengers like myself around the world, telling them she understands what is happening in their lives and that she cares for each of us.

Mary is with her Son, the King of heaven and Earth........... Listening!

Going to Rome

After 2 years of trying to decipher all the information I was receiving, and the impact it was having on me and my family, I decided to seek out even more Priests and Clergy of all denominations to further attempt to establish the validity of my visions.

Were the messages from Mary something that could be further proven and validated to reassure me that I was interpreting the messages accurately? The last thing I wanted to do was unintentionally mislead anyone. I wanted to be sure I acting on Mary's wishes.

I would visit with them the Priests and Clergy and always ask the same question, "Prove me wrong". Is what I am seeing correct in the Biblical interpretation?

On a highly consistent basis, the answer came to yes.

I really hid what was happening to the rest of the world but it was getting more difficult. My family of course knew of my experiences, but I didn't want the judgment and opinions of everyone. I wanted to be as normal as anyone else. It was extremely difficult to hide my true being and experiences.

Mary had another plan.

It was January 1st 2000, and I was in my bedroom changing from taking a shower, when I had another apparition of the Blessed Mother. She told me that I would need to journey to Rome and arrive there at the end of September and remain through the first week of October. Mary told me to go to Mass in the square that was to be held on a Wednesday October 8th. I walked out of my bedroom looked at my husband and said "I have to go to Rome".

I explained the apparition to him and he supported me and agreed that we would save some funds and go.

I planned that trip, knowing that no matter what happened, I had to be there. As my excitement built it became contagious and eventually my entire family wanted to go to and see the wonders and history of the city. All of us including my son, husband, mother and sisters, brothers and their spouses came along.

September came very quickly and upon arrival Rome felt like home to me.

Pope John Paul II was presiding at the time and it was well known of his great devotion to our Lady. As I stood in the square not knowing what to expect with thousands of others, I looked below his window and saw a beautiful picture painted on the wall, yes that's what she looks like. That is a great picture of our Lady.

The Mass Mary directed me to attend turned out to be the Mass of the Visionaries. Along with Pope John Paul, Lucia from Fatima, another great visionary, accompanied him on the altar of the Vatican as they consecrated the bullet he was shot with during a failed assassination attempt a few months prior. This heinous item was consecrated to the Blessed Mother as the statue of Mary was paraded gloriously around the square. It was also the mass of the Bishops. I felt so honored to be there and reveled in the excitement of the traditions and the people thousands of believers in attendance.

As I was standing in the square in the back with my family, I felt that it would be impossible to receive communion due to the vast amount of people in the crowd. But to my amazement, the priests walked around the square and came to me and my family and gave us communion.

Not everyone received communion due to the quantity of the people and we all felt quite blessed. We all walked through the doors to receive a blessing and then went about on our wonderful holiday in Rome; seeing the ancient churches, statues, and artwork that was incredible. And, mostly, meeting some of the kindest and most wonderful people in the world.

If you ever have the opportunity to tour Rome, you will see cathedrals dedicated to Mary and the Apostles - each one providing some manner of proof of their existence and of the reality in which their lives were dedicated to the Heart and Soul of Jesus. Many souls had suffered greatly to prove that there was something more than living and dying on this planet. There was a heaven and Jesus and Mary were a part of something big! It reassured me, as I walked in each basilica and saw the paintings and stories. It was real and it was still happening today.

Could I be proof of that? What is this plan of God? I am the least likely candidate to have such a grace. Many pray all their lives for a sign or a gift or a glimpse of God and here I am………. turned upside down.

The more I accepted my gift, the more I spoke of it in order to help average people with their grief and life issues. Passing the word of Mary to help others became an endeavor that led to several people a day that I was meeting with.

I am still working a full time job as an advertising executive, being a mother to my growing son and, I thought, a good wife. Looking back, it is apparent to me that it must have been such a strain on my family and marriage. Much like a doctor or detective I was taking calls from those in crisis at all hours of the day and night.

My goal began to attempt to do it all and live up to the gift I was given by Mary. Help others where I could help, work as hard as I could, and be there in the evenings for my family. I truly wanted to maintain as much normalcy as possible....... yet normal was still being defined for me.

I would experience many apparitions and stories of providing messages and hope to others in the years to come. On Christmas Eve I always went to midnight mass. But on the Christmas Eve of 2003 I saw My Lord in an apparition in which He told me in Latin that He is the beginning and the end. That He was in control of the world. Every Christmas Eve I receive apparitions from Him. Some are easy and some are more challenging to understand, but I will always try.

I suppose that after a while I could accept Mary's visits to me, but to actually and vividly be visited by Jesus is an experience that I simply can't begin to describe. The glory and majesty that is projected to me is an awesome event that is almost overwhelming.

All-encompassing. To be blessed by His mere presence and even attempt to describe it is impossible to put into words.

As we have discussed, I am beyond the stage of "questioning" any part of this and I thrive on the "knowing" that He is real and that my acceptance is validation that our world is loved and protected. As His warmth radiates within me, I feel every soul and every vision come together as one marvelous event that transcends time and space. He is just everything and everywhere all at once and it makes it seem as though there is so much happening around us that must be realized, understood, and told to the world.

911

The night before the tragedy of 911 that brought our country to it's knees, I awoke to the sound of many people standing in my bedroom. As I looked at their faces, I didn't recognize any of them. As I became more awake, they stood in front of me and then all turned gray and fell to ash. I was extremely startled by this vision, not only by the visual impact, but by not having a clue as to what such a message could possibly mean. My return to sleep after this event was laborious very difficult.

The following day I went to the office at the TV station when the news came out about a plane hitting one of the World Trade Towers in New York. Like the rest of the country we were in shock.

Then the second plane hit the towers. Could this really be happening? I remembered the vision from the night before and, as the day developed, I began to realize what the vision had meant.

People, innocent people, were dying and the towers were turning to ash. Like everyone else I was shocked and worried by the events unfolding before our eyes and recall that afternoon having a make-shift prayer circle at work in an attempt to bring some peace and calmness to those in my office that were so very upset.

My prayer was: "Oh my Jesus have mercy on our sins and save us from the fires of hell".

It blurted out of my mouth and I knew it was the only prayer that made sense at the moment.

The stories began to unfold, families missing loved ones, others at the scene searching for remains of their loved ones. It was such a violent act that impacted so many in the fire and law enforcement community and the families that lost their loved ones who were true heroes in their public service roles.

It also impacted so many in the religious community. Not only were so many innocent lives lost but the families that remained were in need of comfort and grace. From that time forward I decided to help as many people with the Grace I was given. My prayers were to share with families that they are not alone and that their loved ones are in the hands of God.

Off to War

As the war began in Iraq, it was clear to me why this was happening. On a spiritual level, forces of darkness had risen up and had to "re-awaken" the world's need for belief in God and the power of prayer was a necessity to bring all the people of goodwill together.

I soon experienced another vision that clearly showed me 300,000 Kurds buried in the desert north of Iraq. I was told of the spot where we would find the man that did this horrible act and had even drawn a map of the location in my journal. There are many parts of this apparition that I keep private, but my vision much later would prove to be true. At the time I didn't even know what a "Kurd" was nor any military history as to what relevance their slaughter represented.

Like so many visions to come it would be proven true. I was shown acts unfolding in other parts of the world and could see the horror of war and the devastation it had on so many innocent people and families.

The Grotto

January 1, 2004, the Blessed Mother again appeared to me and told me to build an area of worship, known as a "grotto", that was to be a symbol of peace and a place of prayer.

It was to be made out of stones from the farm I lived on and constructed in a specific field on the farm in order to have access to all that may want to come to worship and light a candle in the celebration of love and peace. I remember discussing this with my family and they agreed it was something we had to do.

After much planning and the winter thaw, we started along with many wonderful friends gathering rocks and pulling them by hand or with a chain on a back hoe. Lifting them out of the soil and piling them for further placement. We had picked the spot on a 7 acre field.

We knew this would be a great deal of labor and actually set a deadline of June 24, 2004.

Many friends, and even strangers, joined us in the hard work of moving the vast amount of rocks into their final assembly. As word spread of the Grotto it became a local project with all good intentions and camaraderie of so many working together "one rock at a time". It seemed that everyone that stopped by was thrilled to place "their" rock in just the right spot and say a prayer to Mother Mary. We didn't know why She wanted a Grotto on our farm, we just knew that it was the right thing to do.

It took over 2 months of moving rocks, drilling, digging and arranging to get it completed. It was the year of the Cicada's, an Ohio insect that chose to be a constant annoyance that was not fun to deal with. When you would drill, they would swarm you and hang onto your skin. Maybe they wanted to place their rock also......but they didn't slow us down. We completed the Grotto on June 24th, 2004 and hoisted the statue of Mary that stands there today.

Since the development of the Grotto, word got out it was there. I had people from all over the state and country coming to share in the Grace of Mary. I would spend hours meeting with all walks of people. I listened to their stories and experiences and the sharing about their lives and loved ones alive and deceased.

It became a refuge for some and a private holy spot for me.

To this date that of this writing, over 2000 people have visited the Grotto, each with their own purpose or quest for insight into their specific needs and thoughts that they wish to share with Mary's loving oversight.

All receiving a Grace and all experiencing the love of Mary in their own special manner.

Rosaries and prayers have been said by all faiths at the Grotto and all are welcome to experience what has become accepted as a private spiritual place on earth. The Grotto has even been blessed by Priests and Ministers

I have neighbors who graciously take care of and tend the Grotto, having it always ready to accept the next person into its love and private spiritual embrace.

I now live in Columbus Ohio and visit the Grotto whenever I can. Many friends and strangers meet me at this special place. I pray for Grace before I arrive and I am always amazed at the Grace that is delivered to not only me, but to so many others.

I believe it is important for my reader to understand what I see as I meet with families. The first thing I ask of them is to not tell me anything about their situation prior to our meeting. This would include details of a person's death or details of an illness of a loved one and so on.

Sometimes I will ask who they are seeking, but I let my gift determine what I am seeing. I often describe the visual I am seeing as if it is a sunny day and you see a reflection in a window of a person standing next to you. If you notice with a reflection, you get most of the details but not all.

For me the challenge is describing that reflection. What are they wearing, are they tall or short, average build, hair color and the general look of the person who has passed.

But rather than being in a window reflection, they are standing next to me telling me of their journey in life and in death. It is important to say that no two "contacts" are alike and that each soul is different in a variety of ways. They will share with me what they feel they want to share and not always answer questions that I might have.

You can ask questions and I will do my best to get the answers, however it is the free will of the soul I am connecting with that decides what is communicated to me.

As I am describing the visions I receive to family or friends, it is always the description that allows me to connect with them on earth.

Unfortunately, names are difficult and many times I feel this makes communication more difficult to validate and understand. I have found that if a vision is stating their name, it is to really push a message and declare who they are. But names are given to us on this earth and are not so significant in heaven. I then proceed with talking with the soul that is in front of me.

Often you will see my expression shift or head tilt in a questioning manner as I don't understand why they would tell me of a situation.

An example of this would be a family I consoled just tonight. The woman that had passed to me was wearing a full skirt and white top. It looked of an era past and wasn't something I would expect her to be wearing.

As I told the family that she is in this particular outfit, one of the family members said that the day she died a friend had given her a picture of her mother and she was indeed in that outfit in the picture and it was from the 60's and how wonderful her mother looked in the photograph.

I also will begin to tell the family what they are saying to me rather than have the family tell me of the details as stated before. I do this to confirm without question that indeed I am seeing their family member or friend. Usually, it seems, they are the simple and seemingly insignificant messages that are often shared from the soul of the person that make the most sense.

Many times it will be the personality, style, job, hobbies that are shared that made that person even more unique in life that we all take for granted. As an example, in my conversations I will see that they appreciated the brushing of their hair that was done by a particular family member or that someone had a tattoo in a certain spot on the body. It can be how they loved to cook and a certain food they liked to prepare for others.

These simple things that identify their uniqueness on earth provide validation to the family that I have "connected" with the right person.

When I am describing how a person died and what happened at death, I very often see the same thing. I see the soul looking at their body and maybe the people in the room with them at their time of passing.

They are then escorted by a previously deceased family member, Angel of God and their Guardian Angel that has been accompanying them all through life. They are divinely escorted to Christ and God where they are asked if they believe.

I have to say I have only seen several cases where the soul had to think about it. If they do want to think about it, they are given that opportunity. Sounds odd but I believe that this is the moment of truth and truth of the soul.

As you might guess, I am a Catholic and that might be why I see the way I see for my comprehension. Regardless, that is how I see it over and over again. The feeling of total love as being immersed in a cloud of the love emotion is with the soul in heaven. I call it the "WOW period" at the point when families are amazed and happy with the message I deliver.

I can best describe heaven as a room with all of your family that have died before you in this room. I really don't see beyond this room, maybe because that "WOW" is still waiting for me. As each family member or friend comes forward, I speak with them and try to interpret the best I can to tell the message that the soul wants to share with their loved ones still on the Earth.

I can't say I am channeling or any new age term as I am not sure what all that means. I can say that I can spend as little as a few minutes up to hours with a soul and speak to the family of the messages that are sent.

Many times people will ask if they, the person on earth, is forgiven or if the one who has passed is upset or mad at them. Of course not! But they will try and help them understand the beauty and joy they are experiencing in the afterlife..

Going back to the stories, some are so funny, some are just sweet and caring. Remember how I stated that it's the insignificant messages that mean the most? I have met with families where, for example, I will tell them that the soul was a person who always watched TV in a green recliner and loved to drink beer. In actuality, this is the way to identify who they were. It will connect with the person whom I am speaking with and most of the time stories like this will make us both laugh. Laugh out of joy, grief and connecting to the person that was here on earth.

I find that personalities don't appear to change too much after a person has passed.

I know that when a family is grieving for a loved one how difficult it can be for them. They want to feel that person has changed into a heavenly being or become a better soul in heaven. I really don't see that...... to me, based on all the personalities I have communicated with, what you are is what you are and will remain to be.

You chose in life to be who you are and that personality appears to continue with you in Heaven.

That last statement could scare a lot of people, but it's the truth. I always tell people to live to their fullest. To do what their life and soul call for them to do.

Now I don't mean give up everything and throw caution to the wind.

I mean think of your day and think of those around you and how you impact those around you. Will you be known as kind and compassionate or upset and angry? This is all up to you.

Know that your soul is like a computer downloading all your life's emotions and experiences. It is a part of you like a white wisp flowing constantly inside your body, storing all of your information and life experiences.

My gift has blessed me with the ability to see this "white wisp" and view into the body on what science would call the cellular level. At times I am able to determine whether a person is sick or healthy and the nature of their illness.

Very recently, scientific research has suggested that there is indeed a white wisp of DNA in the body and I have to say I was thrilled when I heard this. It was confirmation for me that indeed what I was seeing could actually be verified.

I wish I could say I could heal the illnesses in a person but that is not a gift I have been given. I only can point out that a person might want to get something I have detected checked out by a physician.

If you have a disease like diabetes for example, it will give me a certain taste in my mouth. I know that must sound so strange and believe me when I say I don't like the taste. But at least it may be an indicator to the person that something isn't quite right and they may need to pay further attention to a medical situation. It's the white wisp we carry that carries with us when we die. It is the energy of our bodies – it is our soul.

When I meet with people, the message may go in multiple directions. I have on numerous occasions seen pets that we have loved in heaven. I may also see other forms of nature and animals that may have been important or part of the family here.

Once I was speaking with a family and interpreting a message from their loved one when I saw a cat walking around his feet. I mentioned the cat to the family and with amazement they said, "Dad hated that cat! Why would he be with Dad?"

The answer is the same, it is a confirmation that all is ok. That even the animals that were a part of the family and loved by the family are at a place of peace and joy waiting for us. Dad may not have loved the cat, but he knew that the family did.

I always find that the soul wants to take care of other souls here on earth. To guide, comfort and console friends and family that have been left behind. It really is very touching and hard to put into words the feeling I have or want to express. Many times they want to hug and kiss the person I am speaking with, that can be very awkward for me as the messenger in this communication. I just have to do my best to describe it in words, it's not my feeling but the emotion being shared to me from souls on the other side.

My Pleasure!

Those are two words I find myself saying quite a bit to people. What I should really be saying is that it is such an honor to function as the bridge of this communication and see the comfort this gift can bring to grieving families. I have learned so much about human nature and grief. I know that we don't take enough time to grieve the passing of our loved ones and reach the "knowing" that they are still with us in just a different way.

As an example, many cultures have traditions such as wearing black arm bands to signify that a person is grieving for a loved one or a loss. Here in America we are expected to get back to life in 5 days.

Loss is a difficult emotion for the world around us to understand and it is sometimes never even spoken of in many families. The feelings are pushed under the rug and left to silent weeping. Yet it is something we all must go through. It is an ache that can't be cured by anything on earth.......just personal understanding and prayer.

I can always tell if a person has faith or been raised with any belief system especially during grief as they have a certain acceptance and inner strength within. I'm not saying it makes it easier to grieve, but more manageable. I always encourage parents of children that are grieving to get them in a faith based community. It will help them not only in their life but help them accept that grieving is ok. It is in our nature to grieve. Faith allows us to believe deep in our souls that the future is ok and that we can get up and move forward with our lives.

I wish I could take away the pain of grief for families, but I can't. Only God will help us in the stages we must go through to allow our minds come to terms with what has happened in our lives. Grieving is not only for someone who has died, it can be for divorce, a job loss, and any changes that deeply affect our hearts. It is as powerful as falling in love and as deep as the ocean. It acknowledges that we deeply cared about a person or life situation. I will be asked, "how long will I grieve?" That is something only you can answer. It can't be rushed and pushed it just takes time.

Special needs

It was a beautiful summer day in Ohio. I was traveling to southern Ohio on a request from a friend to meet with mentally ill and special needs adults.

As I drove, I prayed I could be of help to them and possibly provide some comfort for their disabling conditions and afflictions. I knew this would be a difficult task as most of the adults in the MRDD facility did not speak. How could I help them, I asked Jesus to "give me their thoughts" so possibly I could make a better life even for just one of them.

When I arrived, I was greeted by smiling faces of all ages….. men and woman that had been patients of the facility for years. As I walked down the hall, I met the mothers of these adults eager to have me meet their children. I went to a room and greeted the small crowd and told them that this would be hopefully a happy day for us all.

I met with one man, we will call him John, I asked him if he could stand up and he did. He was about 6 feet tall and of stocky build. Instantly, I knew he was a sweet man that had a lot to say. I could see that he had a form of autism. I asked him if I could touch his head and with two clicks of his right hand he was telling me yes.

You see he couldn't speak and never had. His way of communication was clicking his fingers, one for no and two for yes. I could mystically see the electricity coming from his spine to his mouth and I had the instinct to calm his head. I put my hands on either side of his sweet face and held it for a moment. He clicked his fingers twice and smiled. I wanted to hold him and comfort him. I asked him questions like "does this hurt you or bother you" and he would say no. He smiled. I started to ask him about his day to get answers and to simply communicate. All yes and no answers.

I could see and understand that he was eager to share out of the silence. He told me he loved to sit outside and watch the sunset and that he loved his mother. I also knew that it was difficult for him to eat. I asked the Director of the facility while still holding gently his face, if they were using metal utensils for eating. She said, "Yes why do you ask?"

I also asked if there were others having difficulty in eating. She confirmed that indeed other people were not eating well. I explained that the energy coming through their mouths was reacting to the silverware and making it feel as if they were eating foil. I suggested they get plastic or use wood utensils for the members and see if this made a difference. Back to John.

I spoke with John and calmed his head for over 45 minutes and the time flew by. I looked at his mother who had tears in her eyes and I asked her if I had done something wrong. She looked at me and I will never forget the expression on her face. She told me that no one had touched John for that long of a period. She stated that ever since he was an infant, John was so sensitive to touch that he would cry or agonize of the touch. I looked at John and asked if this was true? He clicked his hand twice. I asked if my holding his head bothered him. And the answer was one click for "no".

We talked, and shared and laughed and later that sunny summer day, John went outside and watched the sunset calmly with his mother.

Later in the week, I heard from the director of the facility. I was advised that they switched the utensils and that the residents were eating much better and how appreciative she was for my input. I think of John often and the special needs that he had. I think of that day and reflect on how a simple change can make such a difference in the lives of people. And I thanked God for giving me the opportunity and the gifts to identify and assist in such beneficial changes. My prayer was answered - one person's life was bettered.

Again, I was called to meet a woman who had questions about her son. I arrived at the restaurant where we agreed to meet. The young boy, Brian, was 4 years old. He was in constant movement and could not speak clearly. He wanted to move all the time. I could see on his mother's face the exhaustion and frustration she had in caring for her him. She clearly loved him and wanted to care for him and make him well.

As I met with her she told me that since Brian was an infant that he has never slept one single night and that his needs were "24 hours a day" and obviously taking it's toll on her.

How exhausting and how difficult it was on their marriage. Nobody can survive on little sleep. As I was talking with her, in my mind I kept seeing "K". Was this the letter K or vitamin K? I pondered and shared with her that I was receiving this message. I knew it was diet related. I knew that it was a situation that could be helped. Actually, I was told it.

I told Brian's mother to check out diets starting with K. Research vitamin K. Something was nagging me about this. She did. She started Brian on the ketosis diet and saw immediate results and often would follow up with me to tell me of his progress. "He's sleeping!", She would say with delight.

She eventually was able to enroll Brian with a speech therapist and put him in programs to help him progress in his abilities the best he could.

Brian is now eight years old. He is in school, speaking, sleeping and leading a normal eight year old life. He shares with his siblings and has wants and needs like every other child. I see pictures once in a while of a happy family sharing their life together. Again it's a small change that can mean so much in a life.

Not all children or adults I see have such experiences, but Grace is a start. It is a chance to begin a new path to health and happiness. I must gratefully say that it is the help of physicians that are willing to listen and have an openness to a new approach that makes the progressive journey to health so effective. Some fine doctors still have the ability to think out-of-the-box after conventional means are exhausted.

So many things in our world are based on the traditional and the "protocol" in the diagnosis of so many ailments. Medicine has made so many advances that are fantastic and have helped so many. I just occasionally ask for the medical community to not forget the importance to spend an extra minute with a patient and hear what is being said.

Recently, I had the wonderful opportunity to speak with a group of prominent physicians about my Gift and the manner in which I relate to people and their sickness and symptomology. I was so pleased with their focus on my presentation and the seriousness that they took my ideas for dealing with certain types of patients.

I feel that being a good detective is the secret that enhances my gift when dealing with issues of illness. Sometimes just spending the time to ask a few additional questions and letting my gift "open and flow" is the secret to "knowing" a potential answer to a problem.

Suicide

I find that we are in a crisis of growing concern. From all walks of life and ages, now amplified by our soldiers returning from the depths of trauma of battle, and including dealing with an entire generation of the exposure to war.

Add to this the feelings of hopelessness of our young people that are being exposed to so much damaging imagery on the Internet to include cyber bullying and violent pornography. Many times, sadly too many to count, I have met with families of loved ones that have chosen to end their own lives.

This story began back in 2002 when a colleague and friend approached me one day while leaving the restrooms at work. My friend asked me in the hallway of the office if by chance I could see her sister in law, Anna that had passed many years ago. She was asking about Anna and stated that she had committed suicide. Although raised in a prominent family, well educated and with a large support system to help her, it was to no avail in stopping her act of devastation.

As I stood and listened to my friend, I realized that yes indeed I could see Anna and immediately "connected" with her spirit.

I felt the overwhelming cloud of sadness surrounding Anna and was told of her agony being conveyed to me that was experienced just before committing the final act. I felt her feelings of hopelessness and frustration and Anna adamantly told me of her deep regret in ending her life from the exact moment that she accomplished the act. She stated that she knew it was a mistake from that very second after the final commitment was made.

Of the many books that delve into the topic with the scientific and medical study of the numerous mental illnesses and analysis involved, I truly think it comes down to one bottom line. This is the "inability to view options" and the false resolution that suicide will take away the pain of carrying a variety of emotions. Sometimes, the person actually experiences "no emotion" and the suicidal act is attempted to "feel something".

There are many different reasons that people choose the taking of their own lives and a discussion of this act of sorrow is not the purpose of my writings. I do feel that if the person was able to view Faith as an option it would, many times, provide a comfort or direction in order to control these feelings within themselves.

Faith might just be the best option of all.

Anna was in heaven. Yet, while communicating with her it felt different as she described it to me. More disconnected and of a different understanding. It felt sad to Anna and that was projected to me. I prayed again for her later that night.

As I talked with my friend I remembered my upbringing and how I was taught that we need to pray for those that have committed suicide. We were taught the fear of where the soul would be were asked to question if it would make it to Heaven. Yet again in surprise, I could see that Anna's soul did. It was there and I could see her in the glory of God as a message to us all.

Anna asked me repeatedly for prayers and forgiveness for her act and was so remorseful for the pain it caused her loved ones that had endured for so many years. Although in heaven, she could still feel the anguish she had caused to her family and children.

This, to be real, frightened me. I had conflict that I knew arose from my religious understanding that suicide was a sin because it went against God's plan for their life. It also created undone grief and self-questioning from all involved. Could more have been done for Anna?

Yes, I feel Anna lacked the option of Faith. The ability to see that life can change and to endeavor to help oneself and others has to remain paramount. This was the message Anna gives now, passed by our blessed Mary.

As I pondered what I was seeing, I prayed and asked for the family to pray for her. Anna could describe her children as they were living in present day. Remember, I didn't know this family that well and the fact that she could reach out and try and help the living was so important.

God is the judge, He is the final destination of all living creatures. He is the one that determines where the final resting place of the soul shall lie. Yes, you get one last chance at free will when you face him after you pass, but he is the judge.

Obviously, some sort of illness of the mind, whether it is long term depression or acute depression as I like to call it. As much as I do not want to discuss acute depression. It is an epidemic in this country.

I am not a psychologist, nor have I studied the mind for decades, but I know what I have been seeing is frightening. It is the act of mind telling the mind to kill itself. I liken it to only having one thought repeated over and over again. It is affecting our youth and in the past year I have been with over six families that have had children involved in acute depression.

I keep searching for the cocktail that is causing this in the minds of our young adults. Some have been prescribed medications others not. Some have been absolutely normal and happy then it hits and they want to end it all. It's so traumatic that the person involved doesn't fully comprehend the outcome and the totality of the ramifications of the act.

Some "succeed" with devastating results, while others end up paralyzed or face years of recovery as a result of their act. All I can say is that God is the judge, he knows our hearts and souls and every hair on our head. He forgives and wants all his children to be with him. Parents suffer tremendously, so do siblings, friends and acquaintances of each person.

Actually, in a very special way, all of mankind suffers from the evil that can be so bad as to take a soul so cruelly.

Some say it is the ultimate selfish act and sometimes it is…….. but not always. It is always a very serious illness that requires a medical or spiritual solution. I have talked with so many about this topic and feel that we, as a society, put so much pressure on ourselves and others to succeed, to have the perfect body, lifestyle, family, job, grades and the list goes on. We have only scratched the surface in dealing with this serious problem of our world.

What we need to put pressure on is love, understanding, faith and yes, to sound cliché, hope. Hope is a beautiful thing, it weathers the storm, it solves immediate crisis and it is grounded in faith. I am sharing this with you, my reader, so that your understanding may mature to acceptance and celebration of our differences.

Remember when I said no two souls look the same? God made us different for a purpose and a reason and is always with us in hope and love.

Ruth

While living at my farm, many people would call and want to come to visit the grotto. They knew it was a very charismatic and spiritual place and that I could possibly answer questions in the heart and souls of those that came. Word got out and more were calling to get answers.

One family had a beautiful daughter that suffered terribly from a shoulder injury and had undergone an extensive surgery that did little to alleviate the problem.

When I first met Ruth I could instantly see that the shoulder didn't heal correctly and had created a "V" of tissue in between the bone and tendons. Ruth was stressed over the pain that it created which was "almost constant".

Of course my first questions involved what she had learned from her surgeon and what the prognosis for healing was. Would further surgeries be necessary and can it be fixed? Ruth advised that the surgeon's opinion was that it could not be fixed surgically and that they had gone to many doctors and received the same opinion. Ruth was looking for answers and wanted to be healed in any way possible without becoming dependant on painkilling medication that promised nothing but short-term relief. At the time she was also going to a natural path doctor and receiving stimulation by electricity in the area of the pain.

Although a good attempt by the doctor, it wasn't working and little improvement was noticed. Sadly, she was confronted with the diagnosis from so many physicians that maybe it was just "in her head" and that she had an "emotional issue" to deal with.

That's not what I saw with Ruth. I saw a person where the only emotional issue was the pain in her shoulder. Sadly, all I could do was assure her that there were no emotional problems and the shoulder was simply not corrected by the physicians. I tried to provide support and give her encouragement that all would be ok and to have hope that the right treatment would be found.

Over a year went by as the agony persisted with no relief in sight. Ruth was frustrated that the pain was affecting her life on a daily basis but continued praying and working with me to find the right physician was all we could do. .

Then one day in the spring of the following year, Ruth decided to go and pray at my grotto. I wasn't there, she went on her own.

As she sat crying in pain, she asked the Blessed Mother for healing and promised that if she were healed that she would serve and help those that had the same problem with understanding and hope.

The blessed Mother must have had a conversation with the divine physician and agreed that Ruth was to be healed. She left the grotto that day never to have pain again in her shoulder. She and I are close, and we both realize the beauty of the Blessed Mother.

She serves her in helping those with muscle aches and pain. She studied the body and became a massage therapist in order to help those in pain. Truly a wonderful example of how a prayer is answered and a life is changed.

As I have stated before, the stories go in all different directions, and now I would like to share some of the divine stories in which I have experienced.

The Eucharist

For those of you who do not know what the Eucharist is, please allow me to explain in layman's terms. It is the final gift Jesus gave to us before his passion and crucifixion. The term itself means thanksgiving and gratitude. As it has been said before "The Eucharist unites with a blessing, the wonders and praises of God". Jesus broke bread and with the apostles at the table, blessed the bread and said "take this all of you and eat this for this is my body, which shall be given up for you".

It is important to understand what transpired that night and why we celebrate the Eucharist. As a young girl receiving my first holy communion, I really thought I understood what that meant. Ok, Jesus is giving us his body in the host that we get on Sunday. Got it! Then as I grew older, and oh so much wiser, I rationally thought that would be really difficult with all the people receiving the host each Sunday around the world. But who am I to question. If it is true, I'm in and if not then blindly I believed. Until one Sunday, while at a very liberal church service things would change for me for the rest of my life.

I was attending at a very liberal Catholic service and it wasn't uncommon for the service to include the arts. For instance, to enhance the beauty of the mass prior to the service they may have more singing or clapping to song. Can we say it was a liberal Catholic service that really is enjoyable? As I stood during the blessing of the bread by the priest, I saw white fog, coming down the aisle of the church. I turned to my son and arrogantly said, what are they doing now? He looked at me puzzled and said "what are you talking about". I said "the fog, don't you see the fog"? He looked at me puzzled. Ok, I thought what is going on? The fog was getting thick around the Alter, how can't anyone see this? Then they appeared! The angels, the big glorious Angels! So startled, I sat back in my chair as if being pushed to sit down. What is going on? Then I saw them follow the Eucharist like bees to a hive. They followed each piece of blessed bread. They followed the person who had ingested the bread. They hovered over them watching their bodies, they left the church with them.

Many months went by as I studied and researched the Eucharist and why we celebrated...... yes that's right, CELEBRATED the Eucharist. Each church I went to the same thing happened. I went to a lot of mass in that six month period. I would get so nervous that I would feel a sense of stage fright before the blessing. Would they be here again? And they always and still are at every blessing of the bread.

My simple conclusion is that they are guarding the body spirit of Jesus. If you could see them the way I do, you too would understand that they are His warriors in Heaven. That they are there to protect and serve.

Often people will ask me, "How long do they stay with you"? The simple maybe innocent answer is as long as the host is in your body. They are his servants, his as we call them Angels that he offers in thanksgiving and gratitude.

Angels

We often hear of Angels and we see what man has put in a statue at Hallmark stores.

But can I tell you that they are fierce and they move at the command to serve and protect. They are strong and bold and they come as messengers, often good and not so good, yet they are terrific and very powerful!

Over the years, I have been a witness to many Angels. There are multiple types of Angels and I get asked quite a bit from people I meet with if they are around them. The answer is yes.

As in the story of the Eucharist, they guard the body and soul of Christ in all of us.

These Angels are huge and white with plates of gold armor on their chests and carry weapons with them to fight the demons that are indeed so prevalent. These are the Angels of spiritual warfare. They are designed to fight and defend our souls from the evil in the world.

They aren't our "guardian Angels" as those are different and I will describe those later.

These are Angels that carry Kopeshis and swords and are given the honor to protect all human beings. Their first commander of course is God but they work at the direction of the Arch Angels that are always at the side of Jesus. They fly with wings that are layers upon layers of feathers. They have a wing span that is large and magnificent like a Condor. They have only one focus and that is to win and to carry their glory toward the goal of the righteous.

Guardian Angels are more human like in form. They are not your passed relatives, but instead given to you at your birth with each being different in appearance and may appear to be more female, male or both in their essence. Modestly dressed in flowing, see through attire, they are yours to ask for guidance and help and often are with you at your death and help guide and nudge you in your life to the right path. I do often see them around people I meet with and speak of them when describing the transition from one life to another.

Arch Angels are truly phenomenal and are with Jesus at all times. They are the leaders in battle and the ones told of in the book of revelations. There are four of them and they serve at the feet of Christ creating the cloud that he always appears upon.

Mary also appears on clouds and it is my belief that she has her own set of Angels to rest her feet and be carried.

I mention Angels to explain what I see. I am often asked if they exist and if they are among us. Based on my so vivid visions the answer is yes.

I feel that people must learn to pray with Angels to guide us and protect us in our worldly troubles. I cannot answer why we all don't see them, maybe it would be too much for us to handle. But with grace, I am permitted to see them and remind all of us that we are not alone.

Mary can utter the command and the world would change. Jesus can say "go" and we wouldn't know what happened to our existence. I am not alone in seeing them, as it has been written thorough the generations that they exist. Always at our side to comfort and defend against evil.

It is hard for me to speak of this, as I am opening myself up to judgment. But I hope you, my reader, can at least hear and conceive of the glory that surrounds each individual.

No one is alone.

Even though we go through trials and tribulations of life, we are never alone.

As I watch the evening news and see suffering all over this planet I often think that it is humans creating this turmoil. Or could it be the dark side in a spiritual battle fighting in the heavens and on earth? That answer is yet to be seen. All I know is that they are messengers that often appear to me in my visions.

The important message I am trying to reveal is that it leads back to hope and faith and Grace. With grace it allows for my day to be normal and enjoyable and allows my humor and life to go forward in normal fashion.

At first when I would have a message for a friend or stranger I kept it to myself and many times still do. I will keep within myself the glory around the person as not to intrude but have faith that all is well.

Occasionally, I must speak out.

As an advertising representative in my daily profession I would meet with clients all day on a variety of business issues On one occasion I was sitting with my client, one of my largest advertisers and I sure didn't want to tell him that a woman buried in pink was standing next to him.

I must have had a strange distracted look on my face as I sat across from him at his desk. My knee started to bounce as the message of the deceased was coming through loud and clear. What do I do? Do I let it go? Do I pretend I have to go to the restroom to escape the experience? I knew this could cost not only my income but what in the world would this man think if I told him. He would think I was nuts!

Praying in my head for the vision to pass, it just got stronger and I questioned what if I'm wrong........ What if he doesn't get it? This was tough.

So calmly I asked, "When your mother passed was she wearing pink"?

My client looked at me with curiosity. I then said, "I know she passed several years ago and I did attend the calling hours but the casket was closed".

Ok, now I am in deep and that didn't come out right as I was trying desperately to be more tactful. He stopped and looked at me and said, "Yes, why do you ask"? I then proceeded to say was she sick with "Alzheimers"? His answer was "yes" and again he wanted to know how and why I would know that. As this was a business appointment, I felt that I was going to be in trouble.

What if my boss heard I was saying this........ I could be fired. But as Grace would lead me, I slowly explained that his mother was standing next to him and wanted to tell him she loved him and that she was ok. He looked to his left and said, "is she standing there"?

My answer was "yes". He wanted to know more and I explained that what I was seeing was a result of a gift that I had. I was still very worried about telling him of my grace.

As I said before, it is like jumping off a cliff and hoping God catches you.

Well I just jumped! And with understanding he knew I wouldn't have any prior knowledge of his mother. This created a bond between us and we still laugh about it today.

He was open to Grace, not by my call but by his own belief in spirituality. I share this story because it is a great example of holding my own knowledge and not sharing versus giving and understanding with compassion that we all have experiences of fear, judgment, and being told what is acceptable and what might be crossing that line.

It gave him comfort and confirmed what I had been experiencing and seeing.

Sometime later, following that experience, I was on a business trip in Las Vegas. All of the sales reps were sitting in the bar having a post meeting cocktail and one of the reps whom I had never met sat in front of me.

By this time word had gotten out that I had "some sort of gift" and, as we were sitting at the small table in the lounge, one of my friends started to discuss my gift, asking questions and wondering about herself and her life.

The new rep was named Cheryl and was sitting across from me when she asked, "what about me". I didn't expect to see what I saw at all and I asked her if she was almost abducted as a child. She was taken aback and confirmed this. Then I saw the man and the car he was driving, the color of the van, the shape and size of the man. As I was speaking, she was immediately confirming everything I said.

I was shocked at what I saw and described where and when and what the man was doing now.

She told me of the frightening experience and all of us at the table were amazed and shocked. Fortunately, it all came forth that she was safe and freed from this potentially dangerous experience that she endured. I wanted to believe that she was protected through this terrible event by her Angels that surrounded her and protected her at the time.

The Soldiers

Have you ever gone to a cemetery and walked the old roads that circle the graves? I have always been curious as to what happened to the people in the time that they were alive.

For some reason it fascinates me. Not to be morbid but just as a curiosity. On Memorial Day, it is a family tradition that we go to the grave site of loved ones and think about their life and how they impacted ours. One year we did just that and started to roam around the Greenlawn Cemetery in Columbus. Greenlawn is a very old historical cemetery with unique monuments to remind us of the life or importance of the person or family.

While at the cemetery we came across an area dedicated to Civil war soldiers and as we approached this area I could see a man in a blue uniform that was wearing a sword and had a horse by his side. He spoke to me with a slight twang of a southern accent.

Surprised and excited, I asked him who he was and was told that he was the "lieutenant in charge" of a brigade of soldiers. He told me that he had led men down to Tennessee and back.

He said that he was "honored by the flag" and wondered why I was wearing the clothes I had on.

I explained that I could see him and he calmly accepted that concept and he spoke of the men he knew and how the women would follow the regiment to feed, help and be with their loved ones.

Then as I was standing in the middle of the graves some saying "unknown" on their tombstones and I could hear their voices. It was apparent that they were Confederate soldiers and some were Union soldiers and that they all wanted to be heard.

Sadly some had died as young men in battle and they told me they were with their families now. Some were from the south and were cynical about being buried in the north however liked the fact that at least their tombstones were identifying them as Confederate soldiers. They spoke of their journeys to Columbus and how many died of disease, wounds, famine and being captured by the Union troops.

The lieutenant was telling stories of the long roads and miles that they had walked. He told me of the need to keep his troops fed and the anguish he felt by the loss of life of his men in battles. The lieutenant explained how fortunate he was to have a horse but that many of his men had walked "literally their shoes off" going into battle. He said that many had lived and died in the cold winters and told of the bravery of his men and how some were buried around him. He was a proud and honorable man with a humble spirit.

Each year I look forward to going to Greenlawn Cemetery and walking to the area of the civil war soldiers, thinking and praying for them and remembering what they went through in their lives to survive. The dedication to a new country being formed and the belief they could make a difference. The lieutenant made a great impact on me with his communication from the beyond.

Camp Chase

Having the experience at Greenlawn Cemetery led me to a different experience and I was later asked by a friend who liked to document the lives of soldiers in the Civil war to pursue this further. My friend asked me to meet him at a place on Sullivant Avenue in Columbus called Camp Chase. We had discussed my experiences at Greenlawn Cemetery and he wanted to hear and see what had happened at Camp Chase.

Even though I was born and raised in Columbus, Ohio I had no clue nor information as to the historical background of the events surrounding the Camp Chase events. I didn't even realize it existed let alone in my city.

We both arrived at the grounds of the area and saw a monument to the Camp that is dedicated to the Confederate soldiers who had lost their lives.

Now how did I miss this in Ohio history let alone in Columbus? As we walked on the grounds my friend took notes on his yellow note pad of what I was seeing and being said to me.

And did I have a lot to say.

Here are some of the scenes and messages I received that day and sadly I wish they were more joyous but they weren't. I could see the fortress around the camp, it was up in the air and Union guards would walk planks of wood from one end to the others carrying rifles ready to shoot any Confederate soldier that created problems.

I could see guard towers on each corner of the fort and then in the back of the site, off the grounds, I kept seeing tents, lots of white tents with soldiers in them as if they were occupying their living quarters. It was muddy, cold and had a foul stench.

The Confederate soldiers began to speak to me of the misery that they had endured during their time in the Camp. Many died of disease and others were killed and died from fighting.

They were buried in the area I was standing in.

I could feel that some of the bodies were placed on top of other bodies and that there were a lot of soldiers that had perished there. I could feel their souls. I could hear how they would write their loved ones back home hoping to survive the conditions of the camp.

Ohio is not known for its mild winters and it was cold, wet and muddy with food being scarce and rationed as most of being shipped out to the Union Soldiers. This wasn't a pleasant place to be.

I was stricken by the number of so many graves.

The Union Soldiers guarding the camp must have hated that duty for they had to endure the suffering and anguish and fear of all the Confederate soldiers placed in the camp under their guard. The camp was much bigger than the plot of land that lies as a memorial to what happened in the Civil war. I could hear the voices of soldiers from both sides complain of the horrible conditions but at least the Union Soldiers could go home or to other accommodations.

This was a time of war and here it was in my own back yard. My friend wrote all the information down and completed many pages on his yellow note pad of the images, feelings, and drama that was conveyed to me that happened at a place called Camp Chase, unbelievably close to downtown of the capital city of our state.

Weeks later, my friend did an investigation of the Camp. He called me and wanted to meet with me to show me pictures and give me a book on what it looked like and the stories from living at the Camp.

It was confirmed, the platform of wood planks high above the ground with the Union soldiers carrying rifles to protect the camp showing the fields of white tents that housed the soldiers. The mud and cold weather and the sorrowful faces of the soldiers that endured the camp were as I had seen to the minutest detail.

Stories of experiences of this nature leave a lasting impression on me and further validate the glory of my gift in not only remembrance but honoring those that passed in a piece of history.

It seems to me that souls cry out to be remembered and not forgotten.

Mathew 25:14 the Parable of the Talents

As I had mentioned early in this writing, when I first received my grace back in 1998 I did a lot of research and strived to be sure that what I was seeing was from God.

I was consistently checking Biblical references for what might be the answers to what Grace was bestowed upon me and I felt I lived at bookstores seeking answers to the visions I had received.

There was one message that kept reoccurring and was first manifest with my Bible.

I would pray before I opened the text and ask for a message that I could understand and relate too. I would then hold the Bible in my hand and allow the pages to open. They consistently opened to Mathew 24:14 the story of Talents.

I would go to any bookstore, home, or anywhere I might happen to come across a Bible and of course it would always open to that passage. The initial amazement of this, like most of the events of my Gift, actually became the norm to me.

At first, I have to admit not being a theologian, I didn't understand. What does this story want to tell me? Why this of all stories in the Bible did it open to this page. It wasn't in the middle of the Bible where bindery would have it easily open to, yet instead it would flip no matter the size of the Bible or it's print to this passage.

At one point I was introduced to, and provided with, a spiritual guide from the church.

Clair is a beautiful nun who was a Jesuit and I would meet with her at least once a month and share my stories.

I started to ask her about this passage that kept "opening" for me and was told by Clair that it is commonly referred to as the "Parable of Talents". The master representing Christ, gives Gifts. Some of us hold them tightly and not sharing the talent. Others go out and say they have a Gift but really don't celebrate or use them to help others.

I believe that mine is like the first servant in the Parable that is given 5 talents who with divine grace shares them in the hope that they will multiply.

This book is one example of sharing my talents and is my way to interpret and express that there is something *more* in this world than what most see. It is about having faith and trust enough that when I share one of the Talents given to me that it will multiply with love for the benefit of others.

This is not easy as there are times when my interpretations fall upon deaf ears.

This, though, hasn't stopped my goal of serving my Lord and Mother Mary.

I patiently, quietly hope that the next experience will multiply. I have shared stories with you that sound very psychic. But in truth they are ways of serving my master, the one true God. I know that many people have many gifts and some of you may see others on the television and hope that they are telling what God's truth is. Many can be found in hospitals aiding the sick and others helping the poor.

I respect the fact that even though it would be easier to ignore them and go about your day, we all choose to reach out and share our talents and do so for the betterment of life.

I am sharing with you how I see The Blessed Mother Mary, the Angels and Jesus Christ. I want to share with you the messages of hope and knowledge of the fact that we are never alone. For the glory behind it is so magnificent. I hope this book will give inspiration for you, my reader, to go and share *your* talents.

It is my belief that if people shared their talents more -embraced faith more - we could have a lasting peace in the world. As I watch the evening news and see all the violence and poverty, I feel blessed and humble. I realize the honor it is to share my gift with people and I hope to always express in the most humble of ways that there is something more to this life on earth. We all live in a stepping stone to eternity and have the free will to make the right decisions in life.

I think sometimes we have to rely on others to pull us up and we need each other as a collective humanity to work together toward a society of belief and love.

It is important to never forget that you too were possibly in a low place, mentally or spiritually and with Grace someone was there to give you their talents and help you through the moment. It can come in the form of a book, a smile, a gesture of kindness. All of them sending a talent ready to multiply.

Romans Chapter 12:5 Many parts but one Body

Again, I must point out another verse in the Bible. This time it sums up what I have expressed with the story of the Parable of Talents.

"Since we have gifts that differ according to the Grace given to us, let us exercise them. If prophecy; in proportion to the faith; if ministry, in ministering, if one is a teacher; in teaching,if one exhorts; in exhortation; if one contributes; in generosity; if one is over another; with diligence; if one acts of mercy; in cheerfulness".

Cheerfulness is something this world could use more of. Many times I meet with people who worry and have anxiety over fears of their "tomorrow."

I know it is so common to hear of people that focus on living in the present "worry" has never accomplished a thing.

Well that's hard to do and I admit it!

I always think of my tomorrow but try to remain in the present.

Our youth that I have met with often ask what their peers think of them and are highly concerned about how they are perceived and accepted in society. Unfortunately, I am coming across more and more teenagers that feel that it is ok to bully another with texting hurtful and destructive messages to their peers. I am seeing this as becoming a real problem in our society and sadly there just aren't enough role models that can help the "bully personality" to see how damaging their words are to others.

In the past year, I have heard of 3 cases of this at local schools and I often ask the teenager if there was a reason behind the offensive and attacking texts.

I am not condemning them or trying to make them feel like it was their fault, simply looking for a rational answer as these actions can place a very deep psychological wound on a person. Some of those preyed upon have confronted the antagonist and have asked for the abuse to stop. That action alone appears to further give a deep sense of power to the bully.

I am bringing this up because this is happening on a vast and unbelievable scale today in our society. After long heartfelt discussions the answer seems to be the same.

Cheerfulness! Forgiveness! Not giving power to the phone or email or the person behind it. Cheerfulness is a powerful tool. It takes the anger and guard away from the source. It says to that person "not me" go away! For I am a child of God with a talent and I am going to spread my talent in service to my Lord and allow psychological attacks to fall along the wayside.

I share this story in hopes that it can heal the anxiety, fear and sadness that so many teens I have been honored to speak with have been burdened by. Teenagers are our hope and future and they need to be nurtured and understood. They seek positive direction from their parents, friends, and society and I don't see them getting it.

Many of our teenagers are growing in a society where they haven't a role model or mentor, they live on the streets in gangs and are holding onto recognition as a way to feel a part of something.

Sadly, this usually doesn't end well.

In my years of meeting with families, I remember one that stands out. This was a family that fostered children from all different family scenarios.

They were a humble kind family that welcomed and truly *tried to understand* the upbringing of each child. They provided a roof over their heads and a warm place to sleep at night. They filled their stomachs with food and attempted to fill their hearts with love and faith. They had talents and they shared them to the best of their capabilities.

Sadly, one night they received the call that all parents never want to receive.

Their foster child had been shot and killed by a gang. He was a troubled teen.

He searched in the wrong place for acceptance and had been in trouble with the law prior to the shooting. I am not saying he was totally innocent, but he was a beautiful young man with so much to offer.

As I met with the family, they wanted to know if he was in heaven and they wanted to know who did this to their child. I could see the situation in a vision and what had occurred. I could see the faces of the shooters and a general idea of who they were. You see, it isn't that I was trying to solve this murder mystery, it was the fact that *God saw it* and He knew who did this crime. It was up to the police to put the pieces together for the family and one day it *will* come together and justice will be achieved.

As for the family, they are trying to live in forgiveness and cheerfulness in honor of their foster son. They *refuse* to give power to the men who pulled the triggers and trust that God will one day make a Judgment as to their actions and assign their fate.

The Police Chief

I was acquainted with a local Police Chief that had spent a majority of his 20 year career in law enforcement focusing on the goal of helping those that could not help themselves. He fought gang activity and spent a nine-year period working undercover in the arrest of narcotics and firearms offenders only to be blocked by society at almost every turn.

The Chief was involved and passionate that those that resided in poor areas of the city truly wanted to find a "way out" and used his "talents" to communicate with younger gang members in an attempt to educate them and find them jobs.

He spoke of the difficulty as the older gang members would become violent when they would see one of "their own" want to "better themselves" and try to pursue an education or gain employment.

It was disheartening to see his amazement that society provided little assistance in all that he attempted. Funding was, and continues to be, reduced in order to make sure tax dollars are spent on the wealthy areas of the Chief's community.

The young that seek treatment assistance with the great influx of heroin are told that they can sign a waiting list - often a nine month venture - in order to receive help.

The Chief grasps onto his spirituality and feels that saving one soul at a time is the only answer and that the problem with a failed "war on drugs" has moved to yet a new generation of complexity and confusion. He views the average politician as egocentric and worried about their "legacy" in the community. Politicians, according to the Chief, are "blind to the truth" of the problems of society.

When he had heard of my Gift, we worked many cases together in an attempt to combine our talents to help an economically depressed subdivision and made quite an impact. After 8 years of reducing crime over 30%, instituting community policing, working closely with juveniles and their families, the Chief was too vocal and was forced out.

When I asked him how he felt about all the work he had done with the community and the fact that it was again quickly slipping back into extreme violence and poverty, the Chief responded that he was "blessed to have had the opportunity" to share his talents and help those that he had over the years. He stated that he had prayed with many people at fatal car crashes and violent shootings and was "honored" to be there to help them "transition to God".

It does not take an army to make a difference to so many - *just one believer* that people can be helped when they are downtrodden or victims of predatory crime and political neglect.

Frustration

I am often asked if having this gift is a burden.

The only time I feel the burden of my gift is when I cannot deliver the message. This has happened to me many times as I have seen world events and been powerless to change or help people involved in them.

It really isn't a burden but more like a frustration and I often wonder why I see these things around the world and yet I have no one to listen to my message or any vehicle to obtain the answers.

This I experienced with the recent devastating tsunami in Japan that created so mush devastation and loss of life for so many.

After watching the reports of the natural tragedy that occurred in Japan on the news, little was yet known of how horrific a catastrophe the tsunami was to the island. The first night after watching what had taken place I went to bed praying for the people of Japan and wishing God to bless upon them the most help and assistance for those families that were literally "wiped out" due to the vast and immediate floods.

But this night I was awakened by the Blessed Mother and she told me to take her hand.

In an instant I was high above the area and viewing the carnage that the water had wrought on the poor villages. I vividly recall the details Mary showed me.

A vast number of cars were covered in mud and debris and were scattered in a horrific mess into what looked like sticks floating in water that once were homes and businesses in this village now obliterated into scrap and debris. It was as though Mary was giving me an aerial view of the entire scene of destruction.

As I watched this horrible scene, Mary showed me Angels going to the cars and lifting the souls from them and carrying them to Heaven. She wanted me to know that She indeed had them with her in a special place and that She was comforting them and taking away their fears and tears and giving them divine love. This looked like hundreds of angels flying to the aid of each soul and was incredible to see.

But then Mary quickly took me to another place in the blink of an instant. This time it appeared to be a factory, or so I thought, and She showed me how water was flooding the facility and that the temperature was too hot in the core of the facility.

This would eventually be revealed to me to me a nuclear power plant.

As astounding as this vision was, Mary sweetly and calmly told me to "put water on it."

I started to worry as I could hear alarms and see gauges and lights that were moving to a red zone. But there is plenty of water around and why put water on it? Was there a fire and I couldn't see the flames? I then sat up in bed in a panic and knew that another disaster was going to hit the Island of Japan.

Over the next few weeks, I saw and heard as well as all of the world, that a nuclear power plant had been compromised and that the tsunami had penetrated the core of the nuclear plant. That brave men attempting to contain the facility were risking their lives to avert a major catastrophe.

They tried several different methods to stop the reactor from overheating and going into a "meltdown" situation, yet I was shown the answer- pour water over it.

The next day I reached out to friends on the west coast and asked if they knew anyone to contact as I was desperate to help. I was told that the Air Force had been notified and that they were monitoring the situation closely with tanker planes. At least there was hope or just another nice way of brushing off my vision.

Weeks later, as expected, the nuclear plant had to be flooded due to damage being so severe. Engineers used the ocean water to cool the reactor.

It wasn't the most environmentally sound thing to do but there were no other options.

As you can see, it isn't a burden to receive messages like this but it is a frustration. I don't know if they would have listened even if I could have actually contacted the company in charge of the reactor.

It was also very reassuring that Mary was there doing her best to save all living things on the planet.

I receive messages from time to time regarding war and disaster and I often ask why these events have to occur and why I must see them with little authority to make a difference in the outcome. I don't get answers to those questions so I must rely on faith and the concept of freewill of man.

I am not saying man causes natural disasters, but maybe it's the greed or arrogance of man that causes freewill to get out of hand. I still ponder the answer and it will be a question someday in my Heaven that I would like to ask.

Wine and Rosaries

In January of 2011, I had a vision of the Blessed Mother in which she told me to start a Rosary group in February. A simple message but a hard thing to do.

I love the Rosary but I really didn't think people would attend my Rosary group. I don't know why......... maybe it was that I felt inadequate to start one due to my not being a devout scholar of religious teachings. Isn't that for the lay people of the church?

I kept envisioning the church lady on Saturday night live starting a Rosary group, who would come?

Please don't misunderstand, I will do whatever Mary asks, however I really thought this was going to be difficult to accomplish. I had to remember to say the Rosary in a proper way with each Docket in order and say it in front of a group.

If no one showed then what would be my next step to get people to come?

And then the idea came to me! We will have wine after saying the Rosary and I'll ask my friends to bring appetizers to share while we discuss various topics and meanings. What I didn't expect was what happened next. I called all my friends and told them of my plan and that we could not only study Rosary but that we could share experiences of Mary and I can answer questions that they may have regarding questions they might have.

I was amazed to see the Blessed Mother show up on each Rosary night. WOW! What a blessing! I would announce as I was starting the Rosary when she would appear. She showed me of world events and personal events for people in my group.

All of the messages are validated!

Word spread that my group met once a month and total strangers started to attend. I didn't care, I was sharing the rosary! Everyone was very welcome.

The Rosary is a series of prayers to meditate on the life of Christ. It is a very powerful tool against evil. Those that recite the Rosary have a special Grace around them. My Rosary group is evidence of this. You would expect all that showed up to say the Rosary would be Catholic, when in fact only a few of us are. Obviously that doesn't make a difference as saying the Rosary is for everyone.

If I counted the people that have been to rosary group over the three years it would be well over two hundred.

People of all ages come, and share. It is a wonderful reflection of the power it has. Some come back the next month and others return when they have a chance. But all involved seem to have a special feeling when they leave. Yes we have ice tea or wine and food following in a fellowship that all are welcome and all is ok for that moment following the Rosary.

Tools

I encourage my readers to look at their lives and see if *you* are in harmony. I really do understand the needs and stress of survival and just trying to be happy. But if we take a moment each day and tell our minds that all is ok, we just need to allow the Grace of God to come in and balance our bodies it will help our families and life relationships.

People need to be loved. It's simple, when we feel love we can accomplish anything. Love gives us the inner strength and courage to deal with our daily problems. It takes the focus off of ourselves and puts it with someone else. Love is a very powerful tool.

In this book I have spoken several times about the powerful tools that God gives us to use on a daily basis to get through the good days and bad days of our lives.

Some of them I often recommend are:

Holy water: Used to keep evil away from our homes and person. It blesses our bodies and helps heal. It is very powerful.

The Rosary: It is a strong meditation on the life of Christ. It can change even the most horrific situations.

Prayer: It gives us that balance and harmony of the mind. It sends a message or a request to be heard by God. When meeting with people I will repeat their prayers back to them to confirm that they were heard. Prayer is beyond a passage in scripture and is a thought for another person that reminds us to keep our spiritual focus in the right direction by working with God through any situation. It is not a wishing well where if we pray we get what we want. Instead, it is beginning of a process to handle all situations.

A candle: Lighting a candle is a reminder of the sacrifices of Christ had at the cross. It is a reminder of all the sacrifices in history and the present.

Holy oils: These oils have extreme abilities to heal the body from infection and virus, and to me there is a reason the wise men brought frankincense and myrrh and gave them as a beautiful gift for health and healing.

Scripture: To give us hope and to show us how our ancestors handled all types of crisis. These writings show us how to pray and the responses we should expect. It provides a record of history for us to learn and remember. Have you ever noticed how relevant scripture is to this day?

I share these with you in an effort to help. I am asked all the time what to do, how to pray, what can I do to help a healing process and these are my tools that I often suggest. None of which can harm but only inspire and help.

These are gifts we are all given to use in our daily lives.

Child of the Corn

One day I received a phone call from a very upset mother. She called with tears in her voice as she had just received news that her son may have lung cancer. He wasn't breathing properly and she had taken him to the doctor. The doctor listened to the boy's lungs and did an x-ray which showed a spot in his lung. The family was frightened and worried of what could would happen next. I wish I could tell you the woman's name but I really can't remember, for I have had so many calls like this before.

Over the phone I listened to the scenario and I was able to see into the child's body and then to the lungs expecting to confirm what the doctors had said, but instead realized that something wasn't quite right.

I asked the mother a simple question, "did your son have corn recently?". She thought and pondered the question with the mother responding with a simple "yes, why?" I kept seeing a kernel of corn that the child had somehow aspirated into the lung. I asked her to go back to her doctor and request another x ray of the lung. She did.

Later that week, I received a phone call from the woman, indeed it was a kernel of corn in the lung of the child. Somehow, and I can't explain how for I am not a doctor, it lodged in his right lung. With medical treatment and a great doctor care, the boy is fine and healthy and happy.

I find that the body will tell you what is wrong in your life if you are ill. I know this may sound silly, but I can look at a persons feet and see the aches and pains and then apply that part to the proper part of the body. I often think about why it is shown to me in this way. I have heard of reflexology and the way different parts of the feet represent different parts of the body and I find this to be true.

As you move up from the feet to the legs and lower groin area this also defines a problem with your foundation. Something has rocked your world and again the body is expressing what sometimes the mind won't allow. We always look for logic and reasoning, yet listening to the body can tell you quite a bit. I have found that when there are intestinal issues they usually indicate issues in relationships with work, family, friends and the list goes on.

Going to the chest area, the heart center and lungs, this can be an indicator of love so deep and love so wrong. Again, stressors that are too much at times to deal with can be *the will* not able to complete its mission.

Chuck

As an account manager for a television station I worked with many clients to have successful campaigns and make sure of the appropriate result for their commercial message. I would meet with the client and have the usual information exchange about their goals and what to expect with their campaigns.

This is my everyday work however this story is a little different. I had met a woman named Margaret and we worked on her project which actually was a very short, one-time television campaign. Not a big project but merely a public service campaign with the local fire department. We worked in October together and met twice, once to discuss what her goals were and the second time to create the commercial. After the commercial was made, it was a matter of phone, email conversations to place media schedule of the project.

But with Margaret it didn't end there as Christmas came that year and she was heavy on my mind.

I felt as though I had to reach out to her after the holidays to check in and make sure everything was going ok for her.

Time passed and it was January 27th. I called Margaret at her office and simply said to her, "you have been on my mind since Christmas, how are you?" I heard in her voice a somber reply "oh yeah". I thought, **well she must be busy** but again I pushed for an answer. Margaret quietly said that she had returned to work that day after having been off since Christmas ands she also told me that it was her wedding anniversary. I wished her my best and wanted to know more as to why she sounded so sad.

As we talked, it was revealed to me that her husband had a heart attack on Christmas and that he passed away on January 17th. . Today was her first day back to work and she told me of all the funeral arrangements that had taken place. At this point I suggested we go to dinner as I wanted to console Margaret and be an ear for her during her time of grief.

A week went by and we went to dinner. Margaret cried and revealed all the details of her husband's passing. His name was Chuck and I didn't know anything about him prior to our conversation. But I knew this was important to Margaret and I wanted to be there for her during her time of grief. Little did Margaret know that Chuck was standing next to our table in a vision and totally clear to me.

As we were sitting at the table, I quietly said to her "I don't mean to pry but your sister, is she alright?" Believe me when I say that is the last thing I wanted to introduce, but I had to tell her. She said all her sisters are fine. I sank back in my chair and again said, one is sick? And she said nope all are ok. I left it at that as I didn't want to offend or make her sadder than she already was.

Months went by and again we met for lunch. It was my way of reaching out to Margaret to make sure she was ok. We sat outside on the patio of the restaurant on a warm spring day. But this time I really could see her sister. She was in a blue dress with a high collar, she was deceased.

Why wouldn't Margaret have told me this? So again I pressed the question "did your sister pass and was she wearing a blue dress with a high ruffled collar"? Margaret had a shocked look on her face as she picked up her cell phone and called a man named Darrel an asked him "was Patty buried in a blue dress with a high ruffled collar"? The man on the other end of the phone replied "yes". She told Darrel she would call him back later to explain then looked at me and said '" My cousin Patty died this past week of cancer, she was buried in the dress you spoke of. She had a closed casket and we didn't know what she was buried in."

Patty was like a sister to Margaret, she lived with Margaret's family growing up. Then it clicked, the night of the dinner, my pressing about the sister and the illness. It all made sense. For Chuck that night told me that he would take care of Patty and was trying to tell Margaret all would be ok

Since that episode, Margaret and I have become great friends and there have been numerous accounts of more messages from Chuck. I got to know Darrel also, and we would share stories regarding Patty and her life.

Sometimes it isn't easy to get answers right away or they may not make sense at the moment. But I always remember this story and remind people to write down what I say as I am speaking to them as the pieces of the puzzle may not be revealed but they will come.

Final Thoughts

As I have shared some of the many thousands of stories I have experienced, I pray that you will find hope and peace and know that there is something more to life than what we experience each day.

This book is a true account of some of the stories that I have personally witnessed as a mystic. I see so many wonderful people and have been honored to be asked to spend an hour of their time as they share their lives and stories.

I know life isn't easy and I can be a firsthand testament for that.

However, as we journey to the end of this experience and move towards our ultimate destination, I hope and pray that when you need guidance and hope that you can turn to this book and realize you are not alone. That something bigger and much more fantastic awaits all of us at the right time.

Never to be rushed or taken lightly, we all have a wonderful purpose for our lives! The fun and challenging experiences we have each day are our choice on how we want to spend our time. God gave us free will because he is not a dictator that controls, instead he is made of pure love for all of us. He wants all of us with him in Heaven at the end of life.

So many times I am asked by people if they will end up in Heaven and the answer is always the same……….. *it's up to you!*

It is your ultimate choice by the daily decisions you make. Yet even if we make bad decisions, God forgives, understands and encourages by sending his messengers to help move us on the right path.

It is understandable to question and try to make logic of our daily experiences and justify why things have happened. That's why we are human. But I ask that we consider the option of recognizing the spirit life.

My journey is different and so intrusive into the spirit life as I have a veil that has been lifted to allow me to serve Mary and *you*. It allows me to offer hope when hope often seems so far away. I just simply listen to the answer, see the situation, and pray for the divine outcome. Guided by Mary the Holy Mother of God, Her Angels, and of course my Lord Jesus Christ, the answers are there.

We know that somewhere within us the answers to everything does exist. It is a matter of listening to them and having the right response to the call of the messengers.

It all began at the Sorrowful Mother Shrine in Carey Ohio. I often recommend that people take their loved ones that are ill or suffering in all sorts of way to the Shrine and pray. When you are there, you will witness the many miracles that have occurred by those attending this lovely holy place. Mary is listening with her son working to help all that take the pilgrimage. This book is an example of the messages received by Jesus himself. He honored me with the presence to encourage and yes even give me a deadline to finish this book. I have made that purpose in my life so that effort will help all of you, my readers. I hope that it will inspire you to know you are not alone.

I am finally enclosing a poem written by a dear friend of mine that expresses hopefully the thought and understanding of what the personal experience is to seek the mystic who had the Night of Mary.

In the Night of Mary

He lost his first love, gone too soon
She found a new love…. Last summer in June
He did not know how to grieve but found peace in the words
She was hopeful about the future but uncertain about the plans
These two people had not met, but shared something in common
They were in search of some comfort
Wondering if God would show them the way
They met a woman with a gift
A mystic guided by faith
They discovered the road
A path to take
The confirmation was proof in the statements she made
Facts about their lives that only she could know
These gifts were like treasures that gave them hope
Sometimes we all need a bit of reassurance
Where are we headed?
Are we are going in the right direction?
People from city to city, amazed by her capabilities
Her apparitions of the Virgin Mary
The ability to see

By Toi Vivo

Made in the USA
Lexington, KY
27 September 2017